I0605696

THE POCKET

Yorkshire English

Published in 2025
by Gemini Books
Part of Gemini Books Group

Based in Woodbridge and London
Marine House, Tide Mill Way
Woodbridge, Suffolk IP12 1AP
United Kingdom

www.geminibooks.com

Part of the Gemini Pockets series

Cover image: Adobe Stock/Vally Images

ISBN 978-1-78675-187-4

A CIP catalogue record for this book is available from the British Library.

Printed in China

10 9 8 7 6 5 4 3 2 1

THE POCKET

Yorkshire English

G:

Contents

Introduction

Modern English was born in Yorkshire! The Anglo-Saxon/ Middle English lingua franca that spread from Yorkshire throughout England is the direct ancestor of the English now spoken all over the world. This handy beginner's guide to 'how to speak Yorkshire' will soon have you giving Sean Bean or Jodie Whittaker a run for their money. You'll be saying, 'Mornin', pet, reet grand day, i'n'it?' in no time!

The dialects of English still spoken in Yorkshire, known collectively as Broad Yorkshire, Tyke or Yorkie, are both colourful and instantly recognisable.

To 'speak Yorkshire', first, you have to drop your Hs, from 'has' and 'her' for example – 'as and 'er. Then, the Ts need to go, from 'that' and 'cat' for example, to be replaced with a slight H sound, the so-called glottal stop – tha' and ca' – while 'the' becomes simply t'. A famous example (which no one ever actually says) is 't'in't in't tin, meaning 'it isn't in the tin'. In a similar way 'with' becomes 'wi'. Accents may differ throughout the Dales, but Ts and Hs are dropped throughout Yorkshire.

And don't bother with the G in any -ing ending. Gs at the end of words count for nothin'. The 'ay' sound in a word, like 'day', becomes 'ee', as do some i sounds – 'right', for

example, becomes 'reet'. So, in Yorkshire, you might say, 'I'm 'avin' a reet grand dee!'

Never say 'our'; you say 'us' – 'Wot's f'r us tea, Mutha?' Yorkshire's a friendly place – anyone you meet could be 'love', 'pal' or 'fella'. And do speak to everyone – you're not in London!

The roots of Yorkshire's dialects can be traced back to the mixing of Anglo-Saxon speakers with Scandivanian settlers from the eighth to the eleventh centuries. In order to understand each other, they dropped gender, word endings and complex conjugations from their languages. The resulting simplified Anglo-Saxon/Middle English lingua franca spread throughout England, more rapidly following the Norman Conquest. Yorkshire is the birthplace of what is now the international language of modern English.

Along the way, the dialects have featured in the work of the Brontës, who were born and lived in Yorkshire, famously in Emily Brontë's *Wuthering Heights*, also in Charles Dickens' *Nicholas Nickleby*, among other classic works.

Yorkshire

–

English

YORKSHIRE	ENGLISH
aboon	above
ackers	money
addle	earn, e.g., 'ows t' 'e addle 'is brass?' – 'what does he do for a living?'
a'gate	do(ing) something, e.g., 'get a'gate' – 'go on then', 'get started at it', 'get doing it'
alike	similar
allicker	old term for vinegar
allock	something which is tiring
allus	always
amangam	amongst them
'appen	perhaps
'appin	bed linen
'appy Larry	someone enjoying themselves (can be used ironically about a sad person)

YORKSHIRE	ENGLISH
'arf baked (*adj.*)	of a simpleton
arrand	spider
arrant	notorious, downright
asker	small lizard, newt
avverbread, avvercake	oatcake, once very popular, but now quite hard to find in Yorkshire, though they are still popular in Staffordshire, where they are known as oatcakes
ax	ask, e.g., 'nivver ax a copper t'way'
axels	molar teeth
aye	yes, especially when beginning an affirmative sentence, e.g., 'aye, it's a fine neet' – 'yes, it's a beautiful night'

YORKSHIRE	ENGLISH
backend	autumn
backword	call off a previous arrangement
badger (*n.* and *v.*)	dealer in flour, cornmeal, etc., also to persistently press someone for information
bagsy	children's callword, as in 'bagsy me first!'
bahn	as in 'weer ta bahn?' – 'where are you going?' and 'weer 'as ta bahn?' – 'where have you been?'
ba'ht	without
band	string
band in t'nick	keep the machine working, literally to make sure that a driving belt is in the pulley
barguest, bargest	ghost, mischievous hobgoblin

YORKSHIRE	ENGLISH
barley	children's truce word used in certain games to claim temporary immunity from capture etc. Many other truce words are found in different parts of Yorkshire, e.g., Barlow, Craven, Kings, Katzen, etc.
barmpot	stupid person
bawson	noisy person
beck	small river or stream
beefin'	crying, complaining
bensel	thrash (someone)
berk	idiot
best bib and tucker	best clothes, dressing up for a night on the town
biddy	louse
bide	like, to wait, e.g., 'ah can't bide that lad ahr Lizzie's courtin''

YORKSHIRE	ENGLISH
billy-o	like the devil, with gusto
birk	birch tree
black bright	very dirty
bleb	blister
blue murder	big trouble
blutherin', blubberin'	crying, weeping
bob	an old shilling; to depart for a short time, e.g., 'ahm just bobbin' out t' t' pub for a quick'n'; to punch. All three senses are used in this ditty about two ex-friends called Robert: 'If thar Bob dusn't gi' ahr Bob t' bob that thar Bob owes ahr Bob then ahr Bob'll bob round t' thar Bob's an' gi' thar Bob a bob on t'nose.'
bobbin	reel for cotton or silk thread, etc.
bogeyed	half asleep

YORKSHIRE	ENGLISH
boggart	ghost, mischievous housegoblin, hobgoblin
boggled	frightened
booit	boot
boose stake	an iron or wooden rod on which a cow chain moves up and down as the cow, which is tied up, moves about
boskin	a wooden, stone or concrete division between each two cows when tied up
bottom	valley, also a person's gravitas
brandrith	container for making Yorkshire puddings
brass	money, e.g., 'wen lads 'ave brass ther're men, wen ther're spent up ther're lads agen'
brat	apron, also a noisy or unpleasant child

YORKSHIRE	ENGLISH
braunging	bragging, boasting
bray	hit hard
breward	brim of a hat
brig o' dread	bridge of the dead that one has to pass over after death, where, according to folklore, one will be helped if one has led a good life but will be hindered if one has committed any sins
brock	badger
bros'n	swollen-headed, literally bursting (after a big meal)
brussin'	stubborn
buck	impertinence, cheek, e.g., 'none o' thar buck, lad!'
buffit	stool
bumblekite	bumblebee
bummerskite	lazy person, a drudge

YORKSHIRE	ENGLISH
butterfingers	someone who drops something or is bad at catching
butty	sandwich
by gum	expression of surprise

black clock

black beetle, cockroach

Cockroaches look much like they did 320 million years ago, according to the fossil record. Their name is a corruption of the Spanish *cucaracha*. Together with termites, they are part of the order Blattodea.

YORKSHIRE	ENGLISH
cack-handed	left-handed
caffle	hesitate
call	gossip, chatter, e.g., 'she's allus callin'' – 'she's always gossiping'
call'oil	gossiping place – this could be a café, a house, a bus shelter or even a backyard
cant	healthy
capt	surprised, astonished, e.g., 'ahm fair capt to see thee agen' – 'I'm rather surprised to see you again'
causiway	pavement
champion	excellent
checkerbrat	woolsorter's overall
chelp	talk loudly, e.g., 'stop thi bairn chelpin', this 'ere's a library' – 'please keep your child quiet, this is a library'

YORKSHIRE	ENGLISH
chimley	chimney
chippy	fish-and-chip shop
chitlins	chicken gizzards (a traditional delicacy)
choose ah, choose ow	no matter how, e.g., 'ah cudn't get the lock undone choose ah' – 'I was unable to open the lock no matter how I tried'
chuddy	chewing gum
chuffed	very excited, very pleased, very proud of or about something
chunterer	grumbler
chumpin'	collecting firewood for Bonfire Night
clap dahn	put something down in a hurry
clawk (*v.*)	claw

YORKSHIRE	ENGLISH
clem, clam	hungry, starving
clever clogs, clever dick	conceited person, know-it-all or simply an insult to take someone down a peg or two
click (*v.*)	snatch at
cloise	field
cod	foreman, supervisor
cog	get a lift on the back of someone else's bike
coil 'oil	coal hole, coal cellar
corporation pop	water
courtin'	going steady with someone, or just going out with them
cracken, crack on (*v.*)	boast
crammocky	stiff-jointed, suffering from rheumatism

YORKSHIRE	ENGLISH
creel	wooden frame hoisted to the ceiling, originally used for drying oatcakes, later became standard in houses to dry clothes
crouterin’	moaning

clock (*n.* and *v.*)

beetle; dandelion in seed; to hit

e.g., ‘ahl clock thee’ – ‘I’ll hit you’; also, ’t’ clock market’ – Halifax covered market; ‘t’ clock almanack’ – the most famous of the Yorkshire dialect almanacs; and ‘under t’ clock’ – arrested by the police and put in the cells

YORKSHIRE	ENGLISH
daft	stupid (along with some other dialect words, such as 'grand' and 'gormless', this has entered standard English)
dander	anger, passion
delf	quarry
delve	dig
din	noise
doff	take off
dog shelf	floor
dollop	lump, piece
dollypeg	plunger for the peggytub, also called a 'peggy-stick'
doy	dear, darling (usually to a child)
easing off	stopping, e.g., 't' rain is easing off'

YORKSHIRE	ENGLISH
'eck!	hell! damn!
ee, een (plural)	eye, eyes
egg on	urge someone to do something (usually something bad)
eller	alder tree
endways	forwards
ey up	hello, how's it going?

deedah

someone from Sheffield

People from Sheffield are famous for pronouncing 'th' as 'd', as in the Yorkshire words 'thee' and 'thou' that end up sound like 'dee' and 'daa', hence deedahs, or dee-dars. Known as Steel City, Sheffield is where Harry Brearley invented stainless steel.

YORKSHIRE	ENGLISH
faffin'	messing about
fain	glad, willing
fair	quite, almost, rather, e.g., 'ah'm fair t' middlin'' – 'I'm quite well, thank you'
fair geffered	worn out
famished	hungry
fettlin'	working, e.g., 'cum on, lads, get fettlin'' – 'come along, everybody, get working'
feckless	useless (referring to a person)
ferntickles, fawntickles	freckles
fill thi boits	enjoy yourself, literally 'fill your boots'
first fooit	first person over the threshold on New Year's Day, an old custom to bring good luck (a 'first fooit' should

YORKSHIRE	ENGLISH
	carry a lump of coal, a piece of bread and a pinch of salt, to signify warmth, food and health for the household for the year to come and should, in return, be offered the hospitality of the house)
fish and fernerkers	fish and chips
flaggin'	wearying
flags	pavement (flagstones), e.g., 'it's crackin' t' flags' – 'it's very hot'
flaid	afraid
flibbertigibbet	chatterbox
flippin'	mild expletive, e.g., 'mi flippin' watch 'as stopped' – 'my damned watch has stopped'
flit	move house
fortyleg	centipede

YORKSHIRE	ENGLISH
fowk	folk, people, e.g., 'ther's nowt sae kweer as fowk', i.e., people do and say the strangest things
fond	a liking for someone, can also imply amorous intentions
frame thi'sen	try harder, e.g., 'frame, laddie, or it's door!' – 'you had better shape up, laddie, or you can go home for good!'
fratchen (*v.*)	argue
friggen' 'ell	supplication to the Norse mother goddess of fertility and good fortune
frummenty	Yorkshire porridge (coarse hulled wheat instead of porridge oats)
fustian	corduroy, moleskin and similar fabrics

forced

sure to be

This is normally used in the negative, i.e., 'I'm not forced to be there', as in the story of the company director, not from Yorkshire, to his staff: 'There is an important meeting on Wednesday and I hope you will all be there,' to which someone from Yorkshire replied, 'I'm going to Hull that day and I'm not forced to be back in time.' Company director: 'It isn't compulsory!'

YORKSHIRE	ENGLISH
gaffer	boss
gallivant	travel about out of town, often used pejoratively to describe someone's uselessness
gallock	left
gander (*n.*)	look; a 'proper gander' is a 'good look'
gannin'	going
gansey	hand-knitted jumper worn by fishermen
gap'oil	gateway
gawp	look, stare
gawby	silly, naive
gear	clothing, bits and pieces
gelt	money
ginnel	passageway between two or more houses

YORKSHIRE	ENGLISH
gi'oer	stop, literally 'give over'
gip	retch
goat	playing around in a childish manner or doing something disapproved of
gob slotch	greedy person, glutton
goff	smell terrible
goosegog	gooseberry
gormless	silly, accident-prone, not very intelligent
grand	great, fantastic, fabulous
gripe	fork
guff	fart
gumption	common sense, horse sense (when it is being emphasised, it is referred to as 'Yorkshire gumption')
guzunder	chamber pot

H I J

H is not much used at the start of words in Yorkshire. Sometimes, when trying to talk 'posh', people overcompensate and put aspirants in places where there is no need. Yorkshire, like German, has silent aitches, so when written down, e.g., 'harkled' (entangled), the h is never pronounced.

hacky	dirty, sticky
ice-shoggles	icicles
i'	in
in a bit	goodbye
in t'	in the
jammy	lucky
jannock	good person, someone sound and reliable
jaunty	flighty
jiggered	tired, exhausted
jock	food, lunch

haver

oats, as in havercakes, or 'avvercakes

The painting, by George Walker, shows a woman making oat cakes. The painting originally appeared in a book called *The Costume of Yorkshire*, published in 1814.

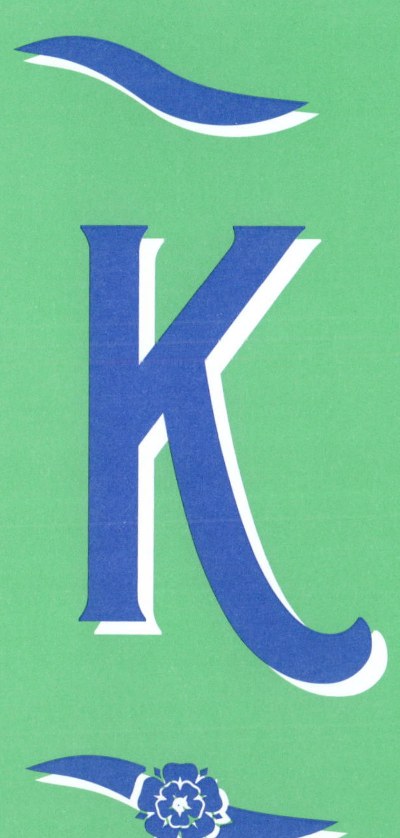

YORKSHIRE	ENGLISH
kag-'anded	left-handed, clumsy
kali (pron. *kay-lie*)	sherbet
kallin'	talking
kegs	trousers
ket	rubbish (referring to useless objects or waste)
ketty	nasty, rancid
kiddin'	joke (to kid is to tell a tall tale with a straight face, the height of Pennine humour')
kist	chest
kit	milk pail
kittlin	kitten
kittle	crafty
knocker-up	person paid to make sure workers woke up in time
kwick	quick

kwacken, quacken (*v.*)

cure

For example, 'a doctor can't kwack a corpse'. The old open-air market in Bradford was nicknamed the 'quack market', a reference to the number of travelling herbalists who used to offer diagnoses and remedies there.

YORKSHIRE	ENGLISH
laik	play (children's games)
laithe	barn
lambasted	struck with force
lamp	hit
lame	painful, e.g., 'by gum, this 'ere tooth's lame today'
lark	good fun
lass	girl, wife, woman
lating	looking for a person
lig	lie, e.g., 'Jack's still liggin' i' bed' – 'Jack's still in bed'
lish	nimble
living ovver t' brush	living together out of wedlock

YORKSHIRE	ENGLISH
loopy	stupid, backward, daft
lop	flea
lowsin' time (pron. *loosin*)	finishing time (at work etc.)
lug, lug 'ole	ear
lugs	knots in hair

liggers

hair combed over a bald patch

It's likely that this is derived from the Yorkshire term ligger, meaning a branch cut and laid down horizontally by a hedger.

YORKSHIRE	ENGLISH
macca	big stone
mad alec	harum-scarum, reckless youngster
maftin’	hot, clammy
manky	bad, foul-smelling, stale
mardy (*adj.* and *n.*)	moody, a spoilt child
marlock (v.)	play about
mashing	brewing (of tea)
mauks	maggots
maumy	off, stale (food)
maungy	sulky, bad-tempered
midden	old-style outside toilet (non-flushable and cleared by night-soil men), e.g., ‘if ’e fell in t’ midden, e’d cum aht smellin’ o’ roses!’ – i.e., nothing sticks to him, figuratively speaking

YORKSHIRE	ENGLISH
middlin'	average
moolah	money
midfeather	removable post to which the two halves of a big barn door are attached when the door is closed
midge	small gnat
millband	string soaked in oil and used to light fireworks etc.
mind	watch out, look after, e.g., 'mind that iron doant fall' – 'watch it! that iron is in danger of falling over' or 'will ye mind ahr Trudy whilst ahr go t' t' corner?' – 'would you look after Trudy whilst I go to the corner shop?'
mindroad	get out of the way
mi'sen	myself
mistal	cow-shed

YORKSHIRE	ENGLISH
mithering	annoying
mobs	horse blinkers (old term)
moorcock	grouse
muck	dirt, e.g., 'weer ther's muck ther's brass' – 'where there's dirt [from work] there is money also' or ''ark at Lady Muck' – 'listen to her, thinking she's so grand'
muck lather	sweat
mud	might, e.g., 'thar mud 'a to do it thi'sen' – 'you might have to do it yourself'
mummer	person dressed up in an unusual costume who goes from door to door on All Saints' Eve (sometimes at Easter) singing a song or, more traditionally, miming
mun	must, e.g., 'thar mun do it thi'sen' – 'you must do it yourself'

to have the monk on

to be grumpy

It's not clear where this expression comes from, but some have suggested that 'monk' is short for 'monkey', as in the expression 'having a monkey on your back', but others believe that it has to do with monks who have taken a vow of silence.

YORKSHIRE	ENGLISH
na then	hello, literally 'now then'
narky	moody, sulky
nay	no
nazard	a horrid or mean person (a particularly nasty person would be an 'arch-nazard')
neb	nose
nesh	cold (referring to the weather)
nick	small, hidden place
nieve	fist (not common)
Nimrod	a term for a friend you're rebuking, e.g., 'ey, Nimrod, 'at's my beer tha's suppin' – 'oy, you're drinking my beer!'
nitherin'	cold
nivver	never

YORKSHIRE	ENGLISH
nobbut	only, e.g., 'it's nobbut a fly, wain't 'arm thee' – 'it is only a fly, it is harmless'
nous	sense
nowt	nothing

nanpie

magpie

A 1954 project to record old Yorkshire names for birds amassed 600 different names for nearly 100 species. The magpie, known throughout Yorkshire as the maggie, is also called the nanpie in parts of what was Yorkshire's North Riding. In many parts of what was West Riding, it is known as the pianet.

YORKSHIRE	ENGLISH
'ob	shelf in front of the fire for the kettle
ocker	hesitate, be indecisive
'od	hold, e.g., ''od on a bit' – 'hold on a moment'; also, 'tak 'od an sup!' – 'cheers!'
oh aye?	oh yes?
'oist	lift, elevator
ornament	decoration, e.g., 'neither use nor ornament' is said of someone who isn't capable of blowing their own nose
oss thi'sen	make an effort
over yonder	over there
'ow do?	how are you?
owt	anything

'oil hole

entranceway, door

There is an old Yorkshire expression, 'put t'wood int' 'oil', meaning 'close the door'.

YORKSHIRE	ENGLISH
paggered	exhausted, broken
parkin	gingerbread
parky	cold
parlour	sitting room, lounge
paupin'	messing about
pawse (*v.*)	kick, e.g., 'if ahr catch 'em, ahl pawse 'em' – 'if I get hold of them, I'll give them a kicking'
peggytub	wash-tub
penker	money
pikelet	crumpet
pine	go hungry, for food or affection
pipsqueak	insignificant or young person
playin' pop	telling someone off

YORKSHIRE	ENGLISH
plot neet	Bonfire Night, 5 November
pobs	bread and hot milk or Bovril and bread
pop	lemonade or similar soft drink
posser	plunger for the peggytub, also called a peggy-stick
powfagged	very tired
pumps	plimsolls, trainers, sometimes refers to dancing shoes

push iron

bicycle

The derivation of 'push iron' is not clear, but one cyclist remembers growing up just outside Hull and calling bikes 'push rods'. Some suggest 'push iron' is actually a Lancashire term.

Q R

YORKSHIRE	ENGLISH

As an initial letter, Q is sometimes replaced by K. There is no fixed rule, but people wishing to appear more educated prefer to emphasise the Q, whilst people who prefer to emphasise the difference from standard English use K.

rapscallion	no-good, troublesome individual
redshank	wooden post between two cows tied up in a mistal
reek	smoke
reet	right
Riding	an ancient administrative division of Yorkshire, created by the Vikings. There were three Ridings, or 'thirds', with their boundaries meeting at the walls of York, until they were done away with in 1974.
roarin'	crying
reycher in	textile worker
rue	regret

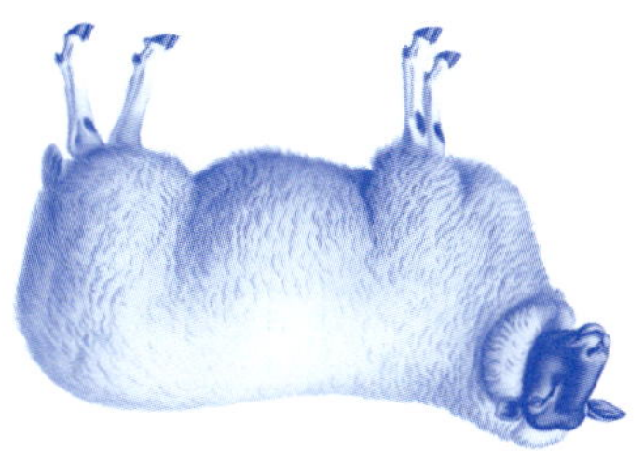

rigwelted

stuck on its back (of a sheep)

The roots of this expression lie in Old Norse, in which 'rygg' means back and 'velte' means overturn. When a sheep has rolled onto its back and can't right itself, which is more likely to happen when a ewe is pregnant, it is said to be rigged, rigwelted or riggweltered. The expression is also used for people confined to bed.

YORKSHIRE	ENGLISH
sackless	clueless
saim	lard (traditionally used for cooking, or, as 'dripping', spread on bread for sandwiches)
sam up	gather, collect
sarnie	sandwich
scran	food
scallions	spring onions
scullery	kitchen
sem't	seemed
session	something done for a while, e.g., 'kallin' session' (chatting), 'suppin' session' (drinking), etc.
set pot	boiler (in a house)

YORKSHIRE	ENGLISH
shepster	starling, e.g., 'Bratford's wick wi' shepsters' – 'Bradford has a lot of starlings'
shippon	cow-shed, byre, mistal
shiverthewink	rascal
silin'	raining, e.g., 'it's fair silin' it dahn' – 'it is raining quite heavily'
sin	since, ago
sitha	excuse me, or look here! e.g., 'sitha, if thee knaws wots gooid for thee, tharl shut it!' – 'excuse me, but I strongly advise you to keep quiet'
si'thee	goodbye, literally 'see you'
skift	move
slapstone	traditional stone sink
slart	splash

YORKSHIRE	ENGLISH
sling	go away, as in 'sling yer 'ook'
sludge	mud
snap	food, especially a packed lunch
snap-tin	lunchbox
sneck	door latch or clasp, e.g., 'put t' sneck on' – 'close the door, please'
snicket	alley, back alley, narrow street
spell	splinter
spiceloaf	currant bread
spogs	sweets
spuggy	sparrow
stalled	tired, bored, weary
stand	long pole

YORKSHIRE	ENGLISH
stand pie	large traditional pork pie
starve	be cold
stoddy	awkward, stubborn
summat	something, e.g., 'summat or nowt' – 'something or nothing', meaning 'nothing important'
sup (*v.*)	drink, e.g., 'we've supped sum stuff toneet' – 'we've drunk a lot tonight'
supwier?	'what is up with her?' (this combination of words into one continuous piece is typical of all northern forms of English)

YORKSHIRE	ENGLISH
ta	thank you
tallyman	door-to-door collector of money, e.g., rent
tarra	goodbye
taws	marbles
tek	take
teem	pour, e.g., 'it's teeming dahn' – 'it's raining heavily'
thackstone	laminated sandstone squares used as a traditional roof covering
think on	think (of), e.g., 'think on wot ahm saying' – 'now remember to think about what I'm saying to you'
thi'sen	yourself
thoil	bear to

YORKSHIRE	ENGLISH
throng	busy, e.g., 'throng as Throp's wife' – 'extremely busy'
tide	fair, festival

tintintin

't'in't in't tin – 'it isn't in the tin'

It should be pointed out that no one in Yorkshire actually says this! Though they might... It's simply a way of illustrating the various common contractions for 'it', isn't', 'in', 'the' and 'tin'.

YORKSHIRE	ENGLISH
tooter	pryer, complainer, nark
twothree	several, a few
topcoit	overcoat
touched (*adj.*)	simpleton, backward person
traps	belongings
trod	garden path
truntlements	odds and ends of little value, the contents of an average boy's pocket
tuskey	rhubarb
tutty	thing, bit of something
twiny	moany
twonk	idiot

YORKSHIRE	ENGLISH
tyke	dog, a low-life person, horse thief, Yorkshireman (depending on context!)

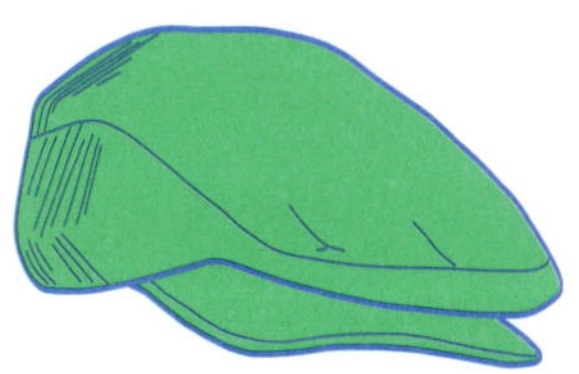

titfer (n.)

hat

The word has derived from cockney rhyming slang, which has migrated north: ‘tit fer tat’ = hat.

Ũ V

U V

YORKSHIRE	ENGLISH
uggeram	carry something for someone, e.g., 'ahm powfagged, can ye uggerem?' – 'I'm very tired, can you please carry these for me?'
'ugger-'mugger	panic, e.g., 'she's i' reet 'ugger-'mugger abaht it, no mistake' – 'she's in a dreadful panic'
'ummer	bother, e.g., 'oh 'eck, there's goin' to be 'ummer' – 'blimey, there's definitely going to be trouble'
un	one
underdrawin'	loft
union shirt	traditional collarless shirt made of cotton warp and woollen weft
us	me, my, our, depending on the context

YORKSHIRE	ENGLISH
usens	ourselves
vary	very
vexed	angry
vittles	food (victuals)

voider

clothes basket

A voider is now a wicker clothes basket, but originally it was a wooden or metal basket or tray used to remove, or 'void', dirty dishes, cutlery and glasses from the table after a meal.

YORKSHIRE	ENGLISH
wang	throw
wark	ache, e.g., 'mi axels dant arf wark' – 'my molar teeth are very painful'
warna	worse than, e.g., ''e's warna a lop' – 'he's worse than a flea' (meaning he's always on the cadge, always wanting to borrow money)
watter	water
way 'od	hang on
wazzock	stupid or annoying person
wed	married
weerzt	where is
wemmel	wobble
wether	castrated lamb
weyvin'	working, e.g., 'cum on, lads, get weyvin''

YORKSHIRE	ENGLISH
whelp	pup
where's tha bin?	where have you been?
while	until
whin	gorse
whippet	dog breed similar to a greyhound once kept for illegal betting races
wick	full of, alive with, lively
wishin	cushion
withy, widdy	metal ring with a swivel to which a cow chain, or tie, is fastened, which runs up and down the boose stake as the cow stands or lies down

YORKSHIRE	ENGLISH
yacker	acre
yam	home
yonder	over there
yon	that there, e.g., 'yon lass is fair cumly' – 'that young woman over there is beautiful'
York'am	cured ham
Yorksher	be smart, sensible, e.g., 'doant try tae pull t' wool ovver mi een, ah's Yorksher too!' – 'don't try to deceive me, where do you think I come from, Lancashire?'
Yorksher Day	1 August, when the white-rose county has the opportunity to congratulate itself and reclaim its historic boundaries established over a thousand years ago

YORKSHIRE	ENGLISH
Yorkshire grit	the hard-headed determination that the people of the 'broad acres' are famous (and infamous) for, a no-nonsense and never-say-die spirit
Yorksher mixture	mixed boiled sweets
Yorksher'oss	horse bought on the black market, or stolen, or simply and more commonly, a fine bit of horseflesh (traditionally a Yorkshire Coach or a Cleveland Bay)
Yorksher parkin	homemade gingerbread
Yorksher relish	a savoury sauce, often referred to as Worcestershire sauce in the rest of the UK
Yorksher teacake	large currant breadcake
Yorksher puddin'	perhaps more commonly known as a 'Yorkshire pudding', this is a savoury 'pudding' made from a batter of egg, flour and milk

English

–

Yorkshire

ENGLISH	YORKSHIRE
above	aboon
accident-prone	gormless
ache	wark
acre	yacker
afraid	flaid
ago	si
alder tree	eller
alive with	wick
alley	snicket
almost	fair
always	allus
amongst them	amangam
anger	dander
angry	vexed
annoying	mithering
annoying person	wazzock
anything	owt
apron	brat
argue	fratchen
ask	ax
astonished	capt
autumn	backend
average	middlin'
awkward	stoddy

B

ENGLISH	YORKSHIRE
back alley	snicket
bad	manky
badger	brock
bad-tempered	maungy
barn	laithe
be cold	starve
be indecisive	ocker
bear to	thoil
bed linen	'appin
been	bahn
beetle	clock
belongings	traps
best clothes	best bib and tucker
bicycle	push iron
big stone	macca
big trouble	blue murder
birch tree	birk
bit of something	tutty
bits and pieces	gear
blister	bleb
boast	cracken, crack on
boasting	braunging
boiler (in a house)	set pot

Bonfire Night, 5 November	plot neet
boot	booit
bored	stalled
boss	gaffer
bother	'ummer
bragging	braunging
brewing (of tea)	mashing
brim of a hat	breward
broken	paggered
bumblebee	bumblekite
bursting	bros'n
busy	throng

ENGLISH	YORKSHIRE
call off a previous arrangement	backword
centipede	fortyleg
chamber pot	guzunder
chatter	call
chatterbox	flibbertigibbet
cheek	buck
chest	kist

chewing gum	chuddy
chicken gizzards	chitlins
chimney	chimley
clammy	maftin’
claw (*v.*)	clawk
clothes basket	voider
clothing	gear
clueless	sackless
clumsy	kag-’anded
coal cellar, coal hole	coil ’oil
cockroach	black clock
cold	nitherin’, parky, nesh
collect	sam up
common sense	gumption
complainer	tooter
complaining	beefin’
conceited person	clever clogs, clever dick
cowshed	mistal, shippon, byre
crafty	kittle
crumpet	pikelet
crying	beefin’, blutherin’, blubberin’, roarin’
cure	kwacken, quacken
cushion	wishin

ENGLISH	YORKSHIRE
damn!	'eck!
darling, dear	doy
dig	delve
dirt	muck
dirty	hacky
do it	a'gate
dog	tyke
door	'oil hole
door latch	sneck
drink	sup
drudge	bummerskite
ear	lug, lug 'ole
earn	addle
elevator	'oist
enjoy yourself	fill thi boits
entranceway	'oil hole
excellent	champion
excuse me	sitha
exhausted	jiggered, paggered
expression of surprise	by gum!
eye	ee, een (plural)

ENGLISH	YORKSHIRE
fabulous, fantastic	grand
fair, festival	tide
fart	guff
few	twothree
field	cloise
finishing time	lowsin' time
fish and chips	fish and fernerkers
fish-and-chip shop	chippy
fist	nieve
flea	lop
flighty	jaunty
floor	dog shelf
folk	fowk
food	jock, scran, vittles, snap (a packed lunch)
foreman	cod
fork	gripe
forwards	endways
foul-smelling	manky
freckles	ferntickles, fawntickles
frightened	boggled
full of	wick

ENGLISH	YORKSHIRE
garden path	trod
gateway	gap'oil
gather	sam up
get out of the way	mindroad
ghost	barguest, bargest, boggart
gingerbread	parkin
glad	fain
glutton, greedy person	gob slotch
go away	sling yer 'ook
going	gannin'
going out with someone	courtin'
good fun	lark
good person	jannock
goodbye	in a bit, si'thee, tarra
gooseberry	goosegog
gorse	whin
gossip	call
gossiping place	call'oil
gravitas	bottom
great	grand
grouse	moorcock
grumbler	chunterer

ENGLISH	YORKSHIRE
hair combed over a bald patch	liggers
half asleep	bogeyed
hang on	way 'od
hat	titfer
healthy	cant
hell!	'eck!
hello	ey up, na then
hesitate	caffle, ocker
hit	clock, lamp, bray (hard)
hobgoblin	boggart
hold	'od
home	yam
horrid person	nazard
horse blinkers	mobs
horse sense	gumption
horse thief	tyke
hot	maftin'
how are you? how's it going?	'ow do? ey up?
hungry	clam, clem, famished

I J K

ENGLISH	YORKSHIRE
icicles	ice-shoggles
idiot	berk, twonk
impertinence	buck
in	i'
in the	in t'
insignificant person	pipsqueak
joking	kiddin'
kick	pawse
kitchen	scullery
kitten	kittlin
knots in hair	lugs
know-it-all	clever clogs, clever dick

L

ENGLISH	YORKSHIRE
lard	saim
lazy person	bummerskite
left	gallock
left-handed	cack-handed, kag-'anded
lie	lig
lift	'oist
like	bide
like the devil	billy-o
liking for someone	fond
lively	wick
living together out of wedlock	living ovver t' brush
loft	underdrawin'
look	gander, gawp
look here!	sitha!
lounge	parlour
louse	biddy
low-life person	tyke
lucky	jammy
lump	dollop
lunch	jock
lunchbox	snap-tin

ENGLISH	YORKSHIRE
maggots	mauks
magpie	nanpie
make an effort	oss thi'sen
marbles	taws
married	wed
me	us
mean person	nazard
messing about	faffin', paupin'
might	mud
mild expletive	flippin'
milk pail	kit
mischievous housegoblin	barguest, boggart
mixed boiled sweets	Yorksher mixture
moaning	crouterin'
moany	twiny
molar teeth	axels
money	ackers, brass, gelt, moolah, penker
moody	mardy, narky
move	skift
move house	flit
mud	sludge
must	mun

my	us
myself	mi'sen

ENGLISH	**YORKSHIRE**
naive	gawby
nark	tooter
nasty	ketty
never	nivver
newt	asker
nimble	lish
no	nay
no matter how	choose ah, choose ow
no-good individual	rapscallion
noise	din
noisy or unpleasant child	brat
noisy person	bawson
nose	neb
not very intelligent	gormless
nothing	nowt

ENGLISH	YORKSHIRE
oatcake	'avverbread, 'avvercake
oats	haver
odds and ends of little value	truntlements
off	maumy
oh yes?	oh aye?
old-style outside toilet	midden
one	un
only	nobbut
our	us
ourselves	usens
over there	over yonder
overcoat	topcoit

YORKSHIRE	ENGLISH
painful	lame
panic	'ugger-'mugger
passageway between houses	ginnel
passion	dander
pavement	causiway, flags
people	fowk
perhaps	'appen
piece	dollop
play	laik, marlock (play about), goat (play in a childish manner)
plimsolls	pumps
plunger for the peggytub	dollypeg, posser
pour	teem
pryer	tooter
pup	whelp
put something down in a hurry	clap dahn

ENGLISH	YORKSHIRE
quarry	delf
quite	fair
raining	silin'
rancid	ketty
rascal	shiverthewink
rather	fair
regret	rue
retch	gip
rhubarb	tuskey
right	reet
rubbish	ket

ENGLISH	YORKSHIRE
sandwich	butty, sarnie
seemed	sem't
sense	nous

several	twothree
sherbet	kali
silly	gawby, gormless
similar	alike
simple, stupid	'arf baked, touched
since	sin
sitting room	parlour
small gnat	midge
small lizard	asker
small river or stream	beck
small, hidden place	nick
smell terrible	goff
smoke	reek
soft drink	pop
someone from Sheffield	deedah
something	summat
something which is tiring	allock
sparrow	spuggy
spider	arrand
splash	slart
splinter	spell
spoilt child	mardy
spring onions	scallions
stale	manky, maumy
stare	gawp
starling	shepster
starving	clem, clam
sticky	hacky
stiff-jointed	crammocky

stool	buffit
stop	gi' o'er
stopping	easing off
string	band
struck with force	lambasted
stubborn	brussin', stoddy
stupid	daft, loopy
stupid person	barmpot, wazzock
suffering from rheumatism	crammocky
sulky	maungy, narky
supervisor	cod
surprised	capt
sweat	muck lather
sweets	spogs
swollen-headed	bros'n

ENGLISH	YORKSHIRE
take	tek
take off	doff
talk loudly	chelp
talking	kallin'
telling someone off	playin' pop

textile worker	reycher in
thank you	ta
that there	yon
thing	tutty
think (of)	think on
thrash (someone)	bensel
throw	wang
tired	jiggered, stalled, powfagged (very)
to be grumpy	to have the monk on
to depart for a short time	bob
trainers	pumps
travel about out of town	gallivant
trousers	kegs
try harder	frame thi'sen

U V

ENGLISH	YORKSHIRE
until	while
urge someone to do something	egg on
useless	feckless
valley	bottom

very dirty	black bright
very excited, pleased, proud	chuffed
very narrow street	snicket

YORKSHIRE	ENGLISH
wait	bide
wash-tub	peggytub
watch out	mind
water	corporation pop, watter
weary	stalled
wearying	flaggin'
weeping	blutherin', blubberin'
what is up with her?	supwier?
where have you been?	where's tha bin?
where is	weerzt
wife, woman, girl	lass
willing	fain
with gusto	billy-o
without	ba'ht
wobble	wemmel
working	fettlin', weyvin
worn out	fair geffered
worse than	warna

ENGLISH	YORKSHIRE
yes	aye
Yorkshire porridge (coarse hulled wheat)	frummenty
Yorkshireman	tyke
young person	pipsqueak
yourself	thi'sen

Yorkshire Idioms

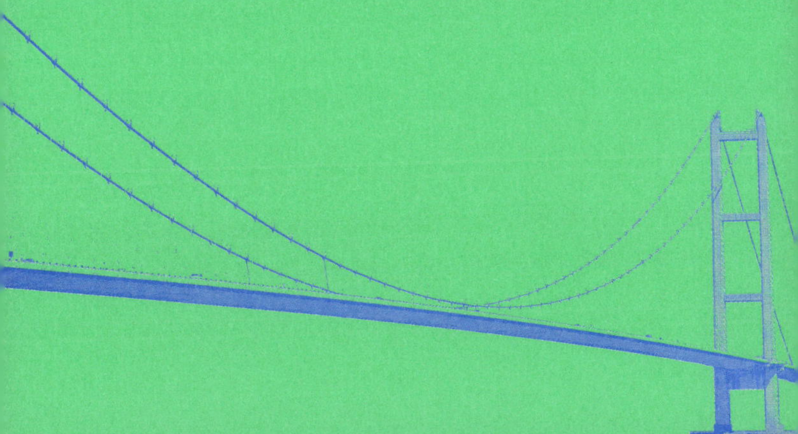

a more jammy so-and-so I niwer met	an inordinately luck person
a reet clogger	a hard man, a fighter
a reet ding-dong	a big argument or fight
as 'appy as a pig i' t' trough	sublimely happy
as 'appy as a sandboy	as happy as a child having fun
as clever as a clog nail	not all that clever
as daft as a dormouse	not very bright
as sharp as Sheffield	quick-witted
as spendthrift as a Leeds loiner	very miserly
catch as catch can	everyone for themselves
clogs'll spark toneet	we'll have a fantastic party/ celebration/night out this evening
don't lost your shirt (i' Skipton)	don't get angry (over nothing)

drop off t' perch	to die
elbow grease nivver did anyone 'arm	hard work never did anyone any harm
'e's not backard at cumin' forrard	pushy or assertive
'e's not sa green as cabbage lookin'	he may look naive, but isn't
from clogs to clogs i' three generations	a family that goes from rags to riches to rags again from grandparent to grandchild; also generally used to describe someone who has frittered away the family fortune
if in doubt, do nowt	if in doubt, do nothing
I'll stand drop o' York	I don't believe it
in't pudding club	pregnant
'is face is like a clog soil	he's not very handsome (literally, his face is like a clog's sole)
lost wi' yersel'	fed up, bored

'od thi' dog back	slow down
'od thi' 'osses	just a minute; stop what you are doing/saying
oop a nick i' bowlin'	mind your own business (if in reply to a question about where someone is) or 'I don't know' (if in reply to a question about where something is)
put t' wood in t' hole	close the door
tha meks a better door than a winder	I can't see because you're in the way
tha mun think on	watch what you're doing
tip over tipple tails	bending over backwards for someone (literally, a backwards somersault)
to pop one's clogs	to die
where there's muck there's brass	where there's dirt (from work) there's money
you can't swing a cat in a ginnel	you can't achieve the impossible

all my and eye and Betty Martin

don't talk nonsense

This also means 'don't lie to me' or 'who are you trying to fool?' Found in British English since the eighteenth century, this expression is less well known today. There is a suggestion that it comes from a Latin prayer, in English, 'Pray for me, blessed Martin', presumed to be St Martin of Tours, the patron saint of innkeepers and reformed drunkards, which is a nice idea, but there is no real evidence for this.

PICTURE CREDITS

Adobe Stock: Vally Images, 3; sketched-graphics, 49; Eric Isselée, 63; Paul Maguire, 67. Shutterstock: Stoker-13, 4; Einstock, 37; Arthur Balitskii, 59; TashaNatasha, 87. Pixabay: completerunner, 7. www.us-now.com: 8, 9, 13. Freepik: Layerace, 27; macrovector, 53; nikapeshkov, 85; fabrikasimf, 91. Wikimedia: R and D Havell, 45; Renee Comet, 121; Krumpi, 127. thegraphicsfairy.com: 75, 110. iStock: pilesasmiles, 122.